BBC

DOCTOR WHO

MAD LIBS®

— BIGGER ON THE INSIDE EDITION —

POLICE PUBLIC CALL BOX

POLICE PUBLIC CALL BOX

T0188651

POLICE TELEPHONE

FREE FOR
USE OF PUBLIC

ADVICE & ASSISTANCE
OBTAINABLE IMMEDIATELY

OFFICERS & CARS
RESPOND TO
URGENT CALLS

PULL TO OPEN

by Rob Valois

Mad Libs
An Imprint of Penguin Random House

MAD LIBS
Penguin Young Readers Group
An Imprint of Penguin Random House LLC

Mad Libs format copyright © 2014, 2018 by Penguin Random House LLC. All rights reserved.

Concept created by Roger Price & Leonard Stern

Previously published in 2014 as *Doctor Who Mad Libs*.
This edition published in 2018 by Mad Libs,
an imprint of Penguin Random House LLC,
345 Hudson Street, New York, New York 10014.
Printed in China

ISBN 9781524793050
3 5 7 9 10 8 6 4 2

MAD LIBS®

INSTRUCTIONS

MAD LIBS® is a game for people who don't like games!
It can be played by one, two, three, four, or forty.

• RIDICULOUSLY SIMPLE DIRECTIONS

In this tablet you will find stories containing blank spaces where words are left out. One player, the READER, selects one of these stories. The READER does not tell anyone what the story is about. Instead, he/she asks the other players, the WRITERS, to give him/her words. These words are used to fill in the blank spaces in the story.

• TO PLAY

The READER asks each WRITER in turn to call out a word—an adjective or a noun or whatever the space calls for—and uses them to fill in the blank spaces in the story. The result is a MAD LIBS® game.

When the READER then reads the completed MAD LIBS® game to the other players, they will discover that they have written a story that is fantastic, screamingly funny, shocking, silly, crazy, or just plain dumb—depending upon which words each WRITER called out.

• EXAMPLE (*Before* and *After*)

"_____!" he said _____
          EXCLAMATION   ADVERB

as he jumped into his convertible _____ and
                                                    NOUN

drove off with his _____ wife.
                         ADJECTIVE

"_____OUCH_____!" he said _____STUPIDLY_____
          EXCLAMATION   ADVERB

as he jumped into his convertible _____CAT_____ and
                                                    NOUN

drove off with his _____BRAVE_____ wife.
                         ADJECTIVE

QUICK REVIEW

In case you have forgotten what adjectives, adverbs, nouns, and verbs are, here is a quick review:

An ADJECTIVE describes something or somebody. *Lumpy, soft, ugly, messy,* and *short* are adjectives.

An ADVERB tells how something is done. It modifies a verb and usually ends in "ly." *Modestly, stupidly, greedily,* and *carefully* are adverbs.

A NOUN is the name of a person, place, or thing. *Sidewalk, umbrella, bridle, bathtub,* and *nose* are nouns.

A VERB is an action word. *Run, pitch, jump,* and *swim* are verbs. Put the verbs in past tense if the directions say PAST TENSE. *Ran, pitched, jumped,* and *swam* are verbs in the past tense.

When we ask for A PLACE, we mean any sort of place: a country or city *(Spain, Cleveland)* or a room *(bathroom, kitchen).*

An EXCLAMATION or SILLY WORD is any sort of funny sound, gasp, grunt, or outcry, like *Wow!, Ouch!, Whomp!, Ick!,* and *Gadzooks!*

When we ask for specific words, like a NUMBER, a COLOR, an ANIMAL, or a PART OF THE BODY, we mean a word that is one of those things, like *seven, blue, horse,* or *head.*

When we ask for a PLURAL, it means more than one. For example, *cat* pluralized is *cats.*

MAD LIBS® is fun to play with friends, but you can also play it by yourself! To begin with, DO NOT look at the story on the page below. Fill in the blanks on this page with the words called for. Then, using the words you have selected, fill in the blank spaces in the story.

Now you've created your own hilarious MAD LIBS® game!

I'M THE DOCTOR

EXCLAMATION _____

NOUN _____

PART OF THE BODY _____

NOUN _____

VERB ENDING IN "ING" _____

ADJECTIVE _____

NUMBER _____

NOUN _____

NOUN _____

VERB ENDING IN "ING" _____

PART OF THE BODY _____

ADJECTIVE _____

ANIMAL _____

PART OF THE BODY _____

NOUN _____

NOUN _____

NOUN _____

COLOR _____

"_____!" I shout as the last of the regeneration energy fades.
EXCLAMATION

Every _____ of my _____ has been rewritten,
NOUN   PART OF THE BODY

and the _____ that I once was is no more. But I am alive, very
NOUN

much so. _____ to my feet, it finally strikes me—what do
VERB ENDING IN "ING"

I look like? Am I _____, or do I have _____
ADJECTIVE   NUMBER

heads? Oh, what about a/an _____? I've never been one of those
NOUN

before. I begin to take inventory of my new _____, starting by
NOUN

_____ my _____. That's odd—it feels
VERB ENDING IN "ING"   PART OF THE BODY

_____ and a little bit like a/an _____. And
ADJECTIVE   ANIMAL

my _____ looks just like a/an _____.
PART OF THE BODY   NOUN

Everything is new, and yet I'm the same _____ I've always been.
NOUN

One thing is certain—I am still the _____! Oh, and my hair,
NOUN

please tell me it's _____.
COLOR

MAD LIBS® is fun to play with friends, but you can also play it by yourself! To begin with, DO NOT look at the story on the page below. Fill in the blanks on this page with the words called for. Then, using the words you have selected, fill in the blank spaces in the story.

Now you've created your own hilarious MAD LIBS® game!

IT'S BIGGER ON THE INSIDE

ADJECTIVE _____

NOUN _____

NOUN _____

VERB _____

EXCLAMATION _____

ADJECTIVE _____

VERB _____

NOUN _____

VERB ENDING IN "ING" _____

ADJECTIVE _____

EXCLAMATION _____

NOUN _____

VERB ENDING IN "ING" _____

NOUN BEGINNING WITH "S" _____

NOUN _____

EXCLAMATION _____

ADJECTIVE _____

It sat in the middle of the field—a/an _____ big blue
                                              ADJECTIVE

_____ . The Doctor says it's his _____ and he uses
     NOUN   NOUN

it to _____ off into space. _____ ! It hardly looks
           VERB   EXCLAMATION

_____ enough to _____ one _____ , never
     ADJECTIVE   VERB   NOUN

mind going _____ around the _____ universe.
              VERB ENDING IN "ING"   ADJECTIVE

_____ ! I've got a bigger _____ at home, but you don't
   EXCLAMATION   NOUN

hear me _____ on about it. He calls it his TARDIS, which
           VERB ENDING IN "ING"

stands for Time And Relative Dimension In _____ . I call
                                              NOUN BEGINNING WITH "S"

it a/an _____ box, because that's what it looks like. Well, into the
             NOUN

TARDIS we go. I still can't see how we'll both . . . _____ ! How
                                                        EXCLAMATION

is this possible? It's more _____ on the inside than it is on the
                                ADJECTIVE

outside.

MAD LIBS® is fun to play with friends, but you can also play it by yourself! To begin with, DO NOT look at the story on the page below. Fill in the blanks on this page with the words called for. Then, using the words you have selected, fill in the blank spaces in the story.

Now you've created your own hilarious MAD LIBS® game!

A NEW DAY

PLURAL NOUN _____

ADVERB _____

ADJECTIVE _____

NOUN _____

ADJECTIVE _____

VERB ENDING IN "ING" _____

NUMBER _____

PLURAL NOUN _____

ADJECTIVE _____

VERB _____

NOUN _____

ADJECTIVE _____

NOUN _____

ADJECTIVE _____

PLURAL NOUN _____

VERB _____

NOUN _____

ADJECTIVE _____

A NEW DAY

It takes a lot of _____ to be the Doctor. It's more than
                    PLURAL NOUN

_____ traveling across space and time in a/an _____ blue
   ADVERB   ADJECTIVE

_____. The Doctor must be heroic, kind, and most importantly,
   NOUN

extraordinarily _____. After _____ the universe
                  ADJECTIVE   VERB ENDING IN "ING"

for over _____ centuries, the Doctor has met innumerable
            NUMBER

_____. Each one has their own _____ story about the
  PLURAL NOUN   ADJECTIVE

Doctor's remarkable ability to _____. Equipped with nothing
                                  VERB

more than a sonic _____ and a/an _____ grin, the Doctor
                    NOUN   ADJECTIVE

can outwit even the most nefarious _____. The Doctor is both
                                      NOUN

_____ and fearless in the face of overwhelming _____.
  ADJECTIVE   PLURAL NOUN

But it's really the Doctor's compassion, empathy, and ability to _____
                                                                    VERB

that separates this Time Lord from every other _____ in the
                                                    NOUN

_____ universe.
 ADJECTIVE

MAD LIBS® is fun to play with friends, but you can also play it by yourself! To begin with, DO NOT look at the story on the page below. Fill in the blanks on this page with the words called for. Then, using the words you have selected, fill in the blank spaces in the story.

Now you've created your own hilarious MAD LIBS® game!

AN UNEXPECTED ADVENTURE

ADVERB _____

PLURAL NOUN _____

PLURAL NOUN _____

ADJECTIVE _____

A PLACE _____

ADJECTIVE _____

COLOR _____

PLURAL NOUN _____

PART OF THE BODY _____

PLURAL NOUN _____

PART OF THE BODY _____

VERB ENDING IN "ING" _____

NOUN _____

NOUN _____

EXCLAMATION _____

PART OF THE BODY _____

SAME PART OF THE BODY _____

ADJECTIVE _____

The cloister bell sounds as the Doctor _____ pulls on
_____ADVERB_____
_____ and presses the multicolored _____
_____PLURAL NOUN_____   _____PLURAL NOUN_____
on the control panel. Oh great, another _____ landing.
                                        _____ADJECTIVE_____
You brace yourself, hoping this destination will be better than the last

trip to (the) _____ . Suddenly the doors swing open and
              ____A PLACE____
reveal a/an _____ _____ sky and the delightful
            ____ADJECTIVE____   ____COLOR____
smell of _____ . "Come on," the Doctor calls as he grabs your
         ___PLURAL NOUN___
_____ and pulls you into this new world. Looking around,
__PART OF THE BODY__
you spot majestic _____ as far as the _____
                  ___PLURAL NOUN___   ___PART OF THE BODY___
can see. Suddenly, _____ in your direction is what
                   VERB ENDING IN "ING"
looks like an alien _____ creature. The Doctor pulls out
                    ____NOUN____
his sonic _____ and shouts, "_____!" The creature
          __NOUN__   ___EXCLAMATION___
stops and extends its _____ . The Doctor reaches out
                      __PART OF THE BODY__
and shakes the alien's _____ . Oh no—this could get
                       SAME PART OF THE BODY
_____ .
___ADJECTIVE___

MAD LIBS® is fun to play with friends, but you can also play it by yourself! To begin with, DO NOT look at the story on the page below. Fill in the blanks on this page with the words called for. Then, using the words you have selected, fill in the blank spaces in the story.

Now you've created your own hilarious MAD LIBS® game!

WHERE SHOULD WE GO TODAY?

VERB ENDING IN "ING" _____

PERSON IN ROOM _____

ADJECTIVE _____

NUMBER _____

VERB (PAST TENSE) _____

NOUN _____

ADJECTIVE _____

COLOR _____

ARTICLE OF CLOTHING _____

VERB ENDING IN "ING" _____

ADVERB _____

NOUN _____

VERB _____

ADVERB _____

A PLACE _____

The familiar sound of the TARDIS _____ nearby woke
                                    VERB ENDING IN "ING"

_____ from a/an _____ sleep. After waiting
       PERSON IN ROOM   ADJECTIVE

for nearly _____ minutes, the Doctor had finally come back for
              NUMBER

her. She quickly jumped out of bed and _____ out into the
                                           VERB (PAST TENSE)

morning air. In the distance, she saw the familiar blue _____
                                                              NOUN

and the _____ man wearing his trademark _____
            ADJECTIVE   COLOR

_____ . "Come along," he called out. "We need
   ARTICLE OF CLOTHING

to get _____ ." She _____ kept running,
        VERB ENDING IN "ING"   ADVERB

straight into the TARDIS. The Doctor smiled as he pressed a button on

the TARDIS's _____ and asked, "What do you think? Where
                   NOUN

should we _____ today?" She _____ replied,
               VERB   ADVERB

"(The) _____ ."
          A PLACE

MAD LIBS® is fun to play with friends, but you can also play it by yourself! To begin with, DO NOT look at the story on the page below. Fill in the blanks on this page with the words called for. Then, using the words you have selected, fill in the blank spaces in the story.

Now you've created your own hilarious MAD LIBS® game!

EXTERMINATE

ADJECTIVE _____

PLURAL NOUN _____

A PLACE _____

PLURAL NOUN _____

VERB _____

PERSON IN ROOM _____

ADJECTIVE _____

ADJECTIVE _____

NOUN _____

VERB _____

PLURAL NOUN _____

VERB ENDING IN "ING" _____

PERSON IN ROOM _____

NOUN _____

PLURAL NOUN _____

VERB ENDING IN "ING" _____

ADJECTIVE _____

EXCLAMATION _____

EXTERMINATE

The Doctor's greatest enemies are the Daleks. A/An _____
                                                      ADJECTIVE

race of mutated _____ from the planet _____,
                  PLURAL NOUN   A PLACE

these _____ have spread out across the universe in
        PLURAL NOUN

search of worlds to _____ . Created by the sinister _____ ,
                      VERB   PERSON IN ROOM

these _____ beings are encased in a shell of _____
        ADJECTIVE   ADJECTIVE

armor that resembles a metallic _____ . The Daleks _____
                                  NOUN   VERB

across time and _____ , bent on _____ the
                  PLURAL NOUN   VERB ENDING IN "ING"

universe. _____ almost defeated the Daleks once and for all
            PERSON IN ROOM

during the Last Great _____ War. Both the Daleks and the Time
                        NOUN

_____ were seemingly wiped out. However, some Daleks
  PLURAL NOUN

escaped this fate and can still be found _____ the universe
                                          VERB ENDING IN "ING"

with their _____ battle cry, "_____!"
            ADJECTIVE   EXCLAMATION

MAD LIBS® is fun to play with friends, but you can also play it by yourself! To begin with, DO NOT look at the story on the page below. Fill in the blanks on this page with the words called for. Then, using the words you have selected, fill in the blank spaces in the story.

Now you've created your own hilarious MAD LIBS® game!

TIMEY-WIMEY

ADJECTIVE _____

PART OF THE BODY _____

NOUN _____

ADVERB _____

PLURAL NOUN _____

NOUN _____

PLURAL NOUN _____

NOUN _____

NOUN _____

ADVERB _____

ARTICLE OF CLOTHING _____

VERB ENDING IN "ING" _____

ADJECTIVE _____

SILLY WORD _____

SILLY WORD _____

The Doctor leaned against the console with a/an _____
ADJECTIVE

look on his _____ . "That's the thing about _____
PART OF THE BODY   _NOUN_

travel," he said while _____ pressing a few buttons and pulling a
ADVERB

few _____ . The _____ continued to spiral across
PLURAL NOUN   _NOUN_

all of space and time. "Most _____ think time is a strict
PLURAL NOUN

progression of _____ to effect. One _____ leads
NOUN   _NOUN_

_____ to another." He adjusted his _____,
ADVERB   _ARTICLE OF CLOTHING_

as he always did when he was _____ . "But actually,
VERB ENDING IN "ING"

from a nonlinear, nonsubjective viewpoint," he added, "it's more like

a/an _____ ball of wibbly-_____ , timey-
ADJECTIVE   _SILLY WORD_

_____ stuff."
SILLY WORD

MAD LIBS® is fun to play with friends, but you can also play it by yourself! To begin with, DO NOT look at the story on the page below. Fill in the blanks on this page with the words called for. Then, using the words you have selected, fill in the blank spaces in the story.

Now you've created your own hilarious MAD LIBS® game!

VOYAGES IN TIME

PLURAL NOUN _____

NUMBER _____

A PLACE _____

NOUN _____

COLOR _____

PLURAL NOUN _____

SILLY WORD _____

NUMBER _____

NUMBER _____

ADJECTIVE _____

NUMBER _____

PLURAL NOUN _____

VERB _____

ADJECTIVE _____

PERSON IN ROOM _____

SILLY WORD _____

VERB (PAST TENSE) _____

A PLACE _____

The Doctor has visited many _____ of Earth history. Here are
                                      PLURAL NOUN

some excerpts from his _____ -Year Diary:
                              NUMBER

- Year unknown, (the) _____ . I don't remember seeing
                            A PLACE

  a/an _____ this color last time I was here. Were they
              NOUN

  always _____ ? And the _____ , they
              COLOR   PLURAL NOUN

  remind me of _____ . No wonder I only visit once every
                   SILLY WORD

  _____ years.
       NUMBER

- New York, year _____ . Ah, it's always _____ to be back
                      NUMBER   ADJECTIVE

  in New York. Of all the Yorks, I would rank this number _____ . I
                                                               NUMBER

  especially like the way the _____ _____ after a long,
                                 PLURAL NOUN   VERB

  _____ day.
      ADJECTIVE

- Once again I arrive in the court of Queen _____ , or
                                                PERSON IN ROOM

  the _____ Queen as she is sometimes known. Although it
         SILLY WORD

  seems that we may have _____ during my last visit, it is
                            VERB (PAST TENSE)

  always good to be back in (the) _____ .
                                      A PLACE

MAD LIBS® is fun to play with friends, but you can also play it by yourself! To begin with, DO NOT look at the story on the page below. Fill in the blanks on this page with the words called for. Then, using the words you have selected, fill in the blank spaces in the story.

Now you've created your own hilarious MAD LIBS® game!

THE BIG BANG

NOUN _____

PERSON IN ROOM _____

NOUN _____

PART OF THE BODY _____

A PLACE _____

NOUN _____

ADVERB _____

PLURAL NOUN _____

PLURAL NOUN _____

PLURAL NOUN _____

PLURAL NOUN _____

SILLY WORD _____

PLURAL NOUN _____

ADJECTIVE _____

PLURAL NOUN _____

The end of the _____ . It was not the first time
NOUN

_____ witnessed it, and maybe not the last, but it
PERSON IN ROOM

still brought a/an _____ to his _____ .
NOUN   PART OF THE BODY

In (the) _____ , he watched as the last _____
A PLACE   NOUN

_____ faded from existence. He'd seen the beginning of the
ADVERB

universe. He'd looked on as the _____ first formed, and wept
PLURAL NOUN

when the earliest _____ began to take shape. Even when the
PLURAL NOUN

very first living _____ crawled up out of the _____
PLURAL NOUN   PLURAL NOUN

and put down their rocks and sticks and said, "_____," he
SILLY WORD

was there. Still, after watching as they grew and eventually set off across

the _____ , it's always _____ to say goodbye to the
PLURAL NOUN   ADJECTIVE

_____ .
PLURAL NOUN

MAD LIBS® is fun to play with friends, but you can also play it by yourself! To begin with, DO NOT look at the story on the page below. Fill in the blanks on this page with the words called for. Then, using the words you have selected, fill in the blank spaces in the story.

Now you've created your own hilarious MAD LIBS® game!

SONTAR-HA!

ADJECTIVE _____

NOUN _____

LAST NAME _____

NOUN _____

ADJECTIVE _____

VERB _____

PLURAL NOUN _____

ADJECTIVE _____

ADVERB _____

VERB _____

ADJECTIVE _____

NOUN _____

ADJECTIVE _____

NOUN _____

VERB ENDING IN "ING" _____

SONTAR-HA!

Congratulations on agreeing to do battle with the _____
ADJECTIVE

Sontaran _____ . I am General _____ of the Fifth
NOUN   LAST NAME

_____ Fleet. From the looks of you, you are clearly a/an
NOUN

_____ species and will be easy to _____ .
ADJECTIVE   VERB

Compared with all the other _____ I've encountered,
PLURAL NOUN

I would rate you _____ . But because you _____
ADJECTIVE   ADVERB

possess the human weakness known as compassion, you will no doubt

_____ at our hands. Do not feel _____ —it is not
VERB   ADJECTIVE

your fault that you are a weakling and a/an _____ . Sontarans
NOUN

are bred to be _____ soldiers. I look forward to defeating you
ADJECTIVE

on the battle- _____ . Just remember: There is no shame in
NOUN

_____ .
VERB ENDING IN "ING"

MAD LIBS® is fun to play with friends, but you can also play it by yourself! To begin with, DO NOT look at the story on the page below. Fill in the blanks on this page with the words called for. Then, using the words you have selected, fill in the blank spaces in the story.

Now you've created your own hilarious MAD LIBS® game!

THE MASTER

FIRST NAME _____

ADJECTIVE _____

A PLACE _____

VERB _____

VERB _____

PLURAL NOUN _____

PLURAL NOUN _____

NOUN _____

PART OF THE BODY _____

ADVERB _____

NOUN _____

ADJECTIVE _____

A PLACE _____

PERSON IN ROOM _____

A PLACE _____

THE MASTER

The Master was _____'s nemesis and a/an _____
                        FIRST NAME   ADJECTIVE

Time Lord. Like the Doctor, he was born on the planet _____,
                                                              A PLACE

could _____ through time and space, and was able to
              VERB

_____ into a new form to escape death. His goal was domination
       VERB

over _____ and _____ and subjugation of
          PLURAL NOUN   PLURAL NOUN

the _____ race. He was a master of _____
          NOUN   PART OF THE BODY

control and would _____ assert his will by stating, "I am the
                          ADVERB

_____, and you will obey me." The Master claimed to
       NOUN

have few _____ opponents and believed that everyone in (the)
                ADJECTIVE

_____ was his inferior. The only person he acknowledged as an
       A PLACE

intellectual equal was _____. And as such, this person was
                            PERSON IN ROOM

the only thing standing between the Master and complete power over (the)

_____.
       A PLACE

MAD LIBS® is fun to play with friends, but you can also play it by yourself! To begin with, DO NOT look at the story on the page below. Fill in the blanks on this page with the words called for. Then, using the words you have selected, fill in the blank spaces in the story.

Now you've created your own hilarious MAD LIBS® game!

GALLIFREY

COLOR _____

COLOR _____

NUMBER _____

ADJECTIVE _____

PLURAL NOUN _____

A PLACE _____

NUMBER _____

COLOR _____

PLURAL NOUN _____

ADJECTIVE _____

NOUN _____

ADJECTIVE _____

PLURAL NOUN _____

PLURAL NOUN _____

COLOR _____

PLURAL NOUN _____

MAD LIBS®

GALLIFREY

The home world of the Time Lords is a/an _____ and
COLOR

_____ planet _____ light years from Earth. Known
COLOR   NUMBER

as Gallifrey—or the _____ World of the Seven _____—
ADJECTIVE   PLURAL NOUN

it once sat in the constellation of (the) _____ . Residing under
A PLACE

_____ suns, Gallifrey's sky would appear as burnt _____
NUMBER   COLOR

as the morning light reflected off the silver _____ that hung
PLURAL NOUN

from all the trees. On the continent of _____ Endeavour—in
ADJECTIVE

the mountains of Solace and Solitude—sat the planet's capital, known as

the _____ . This _____ city was completely
NOUN   ADJECTIVE

enclosed in a mighty dome made of _____ . Beyond the
PLURAL NOUN

city, the _____ seemed to go on forever with slopes of deep
PLURAL NOUN

_____ grass, capped with _____ .
COLOR   PLURAL NOUN

MAD LIBS® is fun to play with friends, but you can also play it by yourself! To begin with, DO NOT look at the story on the page below. Fill in the blanks on this page with the words called for. Then, using the words you have selected, fill in the blank spaces in the story.

Now you've created your own hilarious MAD LIBS® game!

YOU WILL BE UPGRADED

ADJECTIVE _____

PLURAL NOUN _____

ADVERB _____

PLURAL NOUN _____

SAME PLURAL NOUN _____

A PLACE _____

NOUN _____

PART OF THE BODY (PLURAL) _____

NUMBER _____

ADJECTIVE _____

VERB ENDING IN "ING" _____

ADJECTIVE _____

ADJECTIVE _____

"You will be upgraded," a/an _____ robotic voice said as the
                              ADJECTIVE

sound of several metallic _____ crashed against the ground.
                          PLURAL NOUN

"You will become like us." Closing in _____ were the Cyber-
                                       ADVERB

_____ —a race of cybernetically altered _____
PLURAL NOUN   SAME PLURAL NOUN

whose only goal was to conquer (the) _____ and enslave every
                                     A PLACE

_____ . From the sound of clanging _____ ,
NOUN   PART OF THE BODY (PLURAL)

there were at least _____ of them approaching from all
                    NUMBER

directions. "You are _____ . The human race will be reborn as
                     ADJECTIVE

superior beings." The metallic _____ got louder as the
                               VERB ENDING IN "ING"

_____ monsters closed in. "If you are _____ ," it said,
ADJECTIVE   ADJECTIVE

"you will be upgraded."

From DOCTOR WHO MAD LIBS®: BIGGER ON THE INSIDE EDITION • Doctor Who logo © 2018 and
TM BBC. Published in 2018 by Mad Libs, an imprint of Penguin Random House LLC.

MAD LIBS® is fun to play with friends, but you can also play it by yourself! To begin with, DO NOT look at the story on the page below. Fill in the blanks on this page with the words called for. Then, using the words you have selected, fill in the blank spaces in the story.

Now you've created your own hilarious MAD LIBS® game!

TIME CRASH

EXCLAMATION _____

A PLACE _____

NOUN _____

NOUN _____

SAME NOUN _____

VERB _____

PART OF THE BODY (PLURAL) _____

FIRST NAME _____

VERB (PAST TENSE) _____

VERB _____

NOUN _____

NOUN _____

ADVERB _____

A PLACE _____

ADJECTIVE _____

"_____! This is not good," the Doctor said as we sped through
   EXCLAMATION

(the) _____ . He pulled his sonic _____ out of
   A PLACE   NOUN

his jacket pocket and aimed it at a nearby hovering _____ .
                                          NOUN

The _____ began to _____ into two human-
   SAME NOUN   VERB

like creatures. I saw one of the creature's _____ take
                             PART OF THE BODY (PLURAL)

form. Oh my _____ . It looked just like mine! "Run!"
             FIRST NAME

The Doctor _____ and pulled me away. "That's us," he
         VERB (PAST TENSE)

added. "Well . . . future us. If we even so much as _____ with
                         VERB

ourselves, it will create a/an _____ and could tear a hole in the
               NOUN

space-time _____ ." I _____ looked back at future us,
    NOUN   ADVERB

wondering where in (the) _____ the Doctor was going to get that
              A PLACE

_____ hat.
  ADJECTIVE

MAD LIBS® is fun to play with friends, but you can also play it by yourself! To begin with, DO NOT look at the story on the page below. Fill in the blanks on this page with the words called for. Then, using the words you have selected, fill in the blank spaces in the story.

Now you've created your own hilarious MAD LIBS® game!

SONIC SCREWDRIVER

ADJECTIVE _____

ADJECTIVE _____

NOUN _____

ADJECTIVE _____

VERB _____

NOUN _____

ADVERB _____

NOUN _____

VERB _____

PLURAL NOUN _____

SAME PLURAL NOUN _____

VERB ENDING IN "ING" _____

PART OF THE BODY _____

MAD LIBS®
SONIC SCREWDRIVER

Even the most _____ man in the universe needs a little help now
                        ADJECTIVE

and then. Let's find out about all the uses of the Doctor's _____
                                                              ADJECTIVE

sonic screwdriver.

- A locked _____ blocking the way to your _____
             NOUN   ADJECTIVE

  destination? No worries—just _____ it open.
                                   VERB

- Need to access an alien computerized _____ ? _____
                                          NOUN   ADVERB

  point your sonic screwdriver at the computer's main _____ and
                                                         NOUN

  you're good to _____ .
                     VERB

- The one thing the old sonic doesn't work on is _____ . If you
                                                   PLURAL NOUN

  encounter a creature made out of _____ , you can either
                                     SAME PLURAL NOUN

  give it a good _____ with your _____ or just
                   VERB ENDING IN "ING"   PART OF THE BODY

  turn and run.

From DOCTOR WHO MAD LIBS®: BIGGER ON THE INSIDE EDITION • Doctor Who logo © 2018 and
TM BBC. Published in 2018 by Mad Libs, an imprint of Penguin Random House LLC.

MAD LIBS® is fun to play with friends, but you can also play it by yourself! To begin with, DO NOT look at the story on the page below. Fill in the blanks on this page with the words called for. Then, using the words you have selected, fill in the blank spaces in the story.

Now you've created your own hilarious MAD LIBS® game!

DOCTOR, WHAT DO WE DO?

ADJECTIVE _____

ADJECTIVE _____

PLURAL NOUN _____

ADJECTIVE _____

NOUN _____

NOUN _____

PLURAL NOUN _____

ADJECTIVE _____

PLURAL NOUN _____

ADJECTIVE _____

SAME PLURAL NOUN _____

VERB _____

NOUN _____

NOUN _____

NOUN _____

VERB _____

Being the Doctor's companion can be both _____ and
ADJECTIVE

_____ , but it's not all fun and _____ . Take this
ADJECTIVE   PLURAL NOUN

advice from the Doctor if you want to survive:

• There's something you'd better understand about me because it's important,

and one day your life may depend on it: I am definitely a/an _____
ADJECTIVE

man with a/an _____!
NOUN

• A straight _____ may be the shortest distance between two
NOUN

_____ , but it is by no means the most _____ .
PLURAL NOUN   ADJECTIVE

• Never ignore _____ . Unless, of course, you're _____ .
PLURAL NOUN   ADJECTIVE

In which case, you should always ignore _____ .
SAME PLURAL NOUN

• _____ at me! No _____ , no _____ , no
VERB   NOUN   NOUN

weapons worth a/an _____ , oh, and something else I don't
NOUN

have: anything to _____!
VERB

MAD LIBS® is fun to play with friends, but you can also play it by yourself! To begin with, DO NOT look at the story on the page below. Fill in the blanks on this page with the words called for. Then, using the words you have selected, fill in the blank spaces in the story.

Now you've created your own hilarious MAD LIBS® game!

TIME LORDS

NOUN _____

NUMBER _____

A PLACE _____

PLURAL NOUN _____

ADJECTIVE _____

A PLACE _____

NUMBER _____

VERB ENDING IN "ING" _____

COLOR _____

PART OF THE BODY _____

PLURAL NOUN _____

NOUN _____

ADJECTIVE _____

A PLACE _____

VERB (PAST TENSE) _____

PLURAL NOUN _____

Sure, they invented _____ travel and can live for _____
                         NOUN   NUMBER

years, but what do we really know about the most famous inhabitants of (the)

_____? It was said that the Time _____ had one of
     A PLACE   PLURAL NOUN

the most _____ civilizations in the entire _____ and
              ADJECTIVE   A PLACE

that they ruled for nearly _____ million years. They harnessed a/an
                                  NUMBER

_____ star that was about to become a/an _____
VERB ENDING IN "ING"   COLOR

hole. This was known as the _____ of Harmony, and it was
                              PART OF THE BODY

used to construct their advanced _____. They excelled in
                                     PLURAL NOUN

_____ and had the most _____ academy in the whole
     NOUN   ADJECTIVE

_____. The Time Lords could have _____ forever,
     A PLACE   VERB (PAST TENSE)

but war with the _____ led to their apparent destruction.
                   PLURAL NOUN

MAD LIBS® is fun to play with friends, but you can also play it by yourself! To begin with, DO NOT look at the story on the page below. Fill in the blanks on this page with the words called for. Then, using the words you have selected, fill in the blank spaces in the story.

Now you've created your own hilarious MAD LIBS® game!

I'M JOHN SMITH

NOUN _____

VERB _____

A PLACE _____

PERSON IN ROOM _____

PLURAL NOUN _____

ADJECTIVE _____

ANIMAL (PLURAL) _____

PLURAL NOUN _____

ADJECTIVE _____

VERB _____

NOUN _____

VERB ENDING IN "ING" _____

VERB ENDING IN "ING" _____

ADJECTIVE _____

NOUN _____

Ah, the human _____ . Sometimes the Doctor needs
NOUN

to _____ with the native species during his visits to
VERB

(the) _____ . In order to do so, he often assumes the name
A PLACE

_____ . Blending in with _____ isn't always
PERSON IN ROOM   PLURAL NOUN

an easy task for the Doctor. While he sometimes views the humans as a

bunch of _____ _____ , he clearly respects their
ADJECTIVE   ANIMAL (PLURAL)

indomitable _____ and their _____ spirit. And
PLURAL NOUN   ADJECTIVE

their ability to _____ sense out of chaos—after all, a human
VERB

is a/an _____ of hope, forever _____ and
NOUN   VERB ENDING IN "ING"

_____ . The most _____ thing about the human
VERB ENDING IN "ING"   ADJECTIVE

race is that it only takes one _____ to change the course of history.
NOUN

MAD LIBS® is fun to play with friends, but you can also play it by yourself! To begin with, DO NOT look at the story on the page below. Fill in the blanks on this page with the words called for. Then, using the words you have selected, fill in the blank spaces in the story.

Now you've created your own hilarious MAD LIBS® game!

A CLOSE CALL

SILLY WORD _____

NOUN _____

NOUN _____

COLOR _____

ADJECTIVE _____

VERB _____

PART OF THE BODY _____

PLURAL NOUN _____

VERB ENDING IN "ING" _____

PLURAL NOUN _____

ADVERB _____

ADJECTIVE _____

VERB _____

NOUN _____

PART OF THE BODY (PLURAL) _____

NOUN _____

ADJECTIVE _____

NOUN _____

A CLOSE CALL

"_____!" shouted the Doctor as she ran down the corridor of
SILLY WORD

the space _____ . Behind her, a massive _____ -shaped
NOUN   NOUN

shadow tore across the _____ wall. The alien cried out,
COLOR

"You are too _____ , Doctor! _____ all you want,
ADJECTIVE   VERB

but I'll crush you under my _____ and then destroy
PART OF THE BODY

those _____ you travel with!" The Doctor looked around
PLURAL NOUN

for her missing friends and called out, "Yaz? Graham? Where have you

gone?" "Over here, Doc," called Graham. "We're _____
VERB ENDING IN "ING"

behind this pile of _____." "Stay put!" the Doctor replied
PLURAL NOUN

_____ . "I'll go get the TARDIS. If that _____ alien
ADVERB   ADJECTIVE

sees you, just _____ as hard as you can." The Doctor turned and
VERB

ran directly toward the angry _____ and slid beneath the alien's
NOUN

scaly_____ . She reached for the _____
PART OF THE BODY (PLURAL)   NOUN

that hung around her neck and used it to unlock the door to the TARDIS.

"You're as _____ as a Telosian _____!" the Doctor said
ADJECTIVE   NOUN

as the TARDIS door slammed shut.

From DOCTOR WHO MAD LIBS®: BIGGER ON THE INSIDE EDITION • Doctor Who logo © 2018 and
TM BBC. Published in 2018 by Mad Libs, an imprint of Penguin Random House LLC.

MAD LIBS® is fun to play with friends, but you can also play it by yourself! To begin with, DO NOT look at the story on the page below. Fill in the blanks on this page with the words called for. Then, using the words you have selected, fill in the blank spaces in the story.

Now you've created your own hilarious MAD LIBS® game!

FIRST CONTACT

NOUN _____

ADJECTIVE _____

PLURAL NOUN _____

VERB ENDING IN "ING" _____

PART OF THE BODY _____

ADJECTIVE _____

NOUN _____

NOUN _____

VERB _____

VERB _____

NOUN _____

PLURAL NOUN _____

VERB ENDING IN "ING" _____

NOUN _____

A PLACE _____

ADJECTIVE _____

Meeting an alien _____ for the first time can be _____ if you
NOUN _ADJECTIVE_

don't play your _____ right. Here's a list of things to look out
PLURAL NOUN

for while making first contact:

1. Contact doesn't always mean _____ . For some species,
    VERB ENDING IN "ING"

    a nice pat on the _____ or a/an _____ handshake
    PART OF THE BODY _ADJECTIVE_

    will suffice. Others may view it as a/an _____ of aggression.
    NOUN

    Beware!

2. Gift giving. In some cultures, presenting a potted _____ is the
    NOUN

    best way to say, "Nice to _____ you." But in others it could
    VERB

    mean "_____ away, you _____!" Always read up on
    VERB _NOUN_

    local _____ before visiting.
    PLURAL NOUN

3. Finally, always avoid _____ a/an _____
    VERB ENDING IN "ING" _NOUN_

    when you visit (the) _____ . Unless you want to end up
    A PLACE

    _____ .
    ADJECTIVE

MAD LIBS® is fun to play with friends, but you can also play it by yourself! To begin with, DO NOT look at the story on the page below. Fill in the blanks on this page with the words called for. Then, using the words you have selected, fill in the blank spaces in the story.

Now you've created your own hilarious MAD LIBS® game!

THROUGH TIME

NUMBER _____

NOUN _____

ADJECTIVE _____

PLURAL NOUN _____

ADJECTIVE _____

A PLACE _____

ADJECTIVE _____

PLURAL NOUN _____

NOUN _____

PERSON IN ROOM _____

PERSON IN ROOM _____

CELEBRITY _____

PLURAL NOUN _____

VERB _____

NOUN _____

ADJECTIVE _____

PLURAL NOUN _____

NOUN _____

MAD LIBS
THROUGH TIME

For more than _____ years, the Doctor has traveled through space
                    NUMBER

and time in the magical blue _____. During these _____
                              NOUN   ADJECTIVE

journeys, the Doctor has encountered many _____ and
                                          PLURAL NOUN

visited _____ places like Mars, ancient Rome, and of course
        ADJECTIVE

(the) _____. Along the way, the Time Lord has made many
      A PLACE

_____ enemies like the Daleks, the Ice _____,
ADJECTIVE   PLURAL NOUN

and the Great _____—but has also made many friends, such
              NOUN

as _____, _____, and _____.
   PERSON IN ROOM   PERSON IN ROOM   CELEBRITY

The Doctor's goal has always been to bring _____ and to
                                           PLURAL NOUN

_____ the helpless—even if it means going to war. Throughout
VERB

all of time and _____, the Doctor has maintained one
                NOUN

_____ goal: to always defend the _____—even if it
ADJECTIVE   PLURAL NOUN

means putting life and _____ in the line of fire.
                       NOUN

Download Mad Libs today!

Join the millions of Mad Libs fans creating wacky and wonderful stories on our apps!

POLICE PUBLIC CALL BOX

POLICE TELEPHONE
FREE FOR
USE OF PUBLIC
ADVICE & ASSISTANCE
OBTAINABLE IMMEDIATELY
OFFICERS & CARS
RESPOND TO
URGENT CALLS
PULL TO OPEN

MAD LIBS®

DOCTOR WHO

BBC